THE ALPHABET SAFARI

ZOE HART

THIS BOOK BELONGS TO

_____

_____

In a dusty corner, between old board games and stuffed teddy bears, Alex stumbled upon a gem.

"The Alphabet Safari?!"

he exclaimed.

Flipping it open, to his surprise,
letters jumped out!
'A' suited up as an astronaut, while
a bear chuckled by his side.
This isn't just a book, it's a ticket
to fun ride.
"I cannot wait."

Hey there! It's 'A', not just any astronaut, but one who dreams of cosmic candy bars.

Amidst the pages, a jolly 'B' emerged, as a bear with quite the flair! Look at him go, wiggling and giggling, moonwalking without a care!

Next up, a sly surprise! 'C', the cuddly cat, all snug and smug. Lounging on a comfy seat, humming a purrfectly lazy beat.

Look! It's 'D' for the delightful dog, dancing with joy in front of his beautiful home.

And behold! 'E', the ever-enthusiastic elephant, stepping with zest. Those big, bold ears, like the 'E', she represents at best!

Oh, jump for joy! It's 'F', featuring frogs that flip and fly. With each hop and skip, they seem to touch the sky!

Check out 'G', the giraffe so tall,
laughing and lounging, having a ball!
His long neck gracefully aligns, with
the giant 'G' where he reclines.

And here's 'H', a horse that's neat,
running fast with happy feet!

Iguana 'I', dreaming high,
gazes at the vast blue sky.

Amidst a flurry of
colorful balloons,
the Jaguar named 'J'
shows off ,
jumping so neat,
with a tail like a 'J',
look at those feet!

With a zest for life, 'K' the Kangaroo, always eager, takes a moment before launching into one of her signature high jumps.

'L' represents the Leisurely Lion, basking in the sun with a chuckle, finding comfort in nature's embrace.

'M' is for the Melodic Monkey, dancing through the trees, every move in harmony with nature's breeze.

'N' stands for the Nurturing Nightingale, soaring through the night. With a song so soft and a flight so right, she traces 'N' with her twilight flight.

'O' for the Observant Owl, perched with pride. His round eyes wide, reflecting the world outside, mirroring the shape of an 'O' so wide.

'P' for the Playful Penguin, waddling with glee. On icy shores and chilly seas, he stands tall and free, always resembling the upright letter 'P'.

'Q' for the Quick Quokka, always on the move. With a tail curling like a 'Q', he grooves to his own tune, dancing and darting under the sun and moon.

Rolling in with 'R' is our radiant rabbit, always raring to race. With every rapid hop, he reminds us of the 'R', right in his vibrant place.

Sneaking 'S' is our striking snake, shimmering in the sun's embrace. With each spiral and sway, he shapes just like the 'S', a captivating display.

Here's 'T' for our turtle, so true and tall! With a 'T' on his back, he takes his ime, never in a hurry at all.

U is for unicorn, so unique and bright. With colors that shine and a horn of pure light, she represents 'U' with all her might.

V for Vulture, not a typical birdie,
Resting on 'V', isn't she quirky?
With pinkish hue and a pose so flighty,
In the valley below, she's the party
highlight-y!

Wally the Walrus, all whiskery and wise,
Lay by 'W', with big, surprised eyes!
With seagulls above and waves at his flippers,
He wonders if 'W' tastes like fishy kippers!

Xander the X-ray fish, with bones on display,
Swam near 'X', making bubbles on his way.

Yosef the Yak, with a
yawn and a sigh,
Trailed by the 'Y', under
the bright blue sky.

Alright, kiddo, here's our pal 'Z'! Zane the Zippy Zebra, with a zoom and a zap. See his stripes going zig and zag? He's the last to say 'hi', but with a zip and a zap, he's never too shy!

Phew, what a journey! As the last page turned, the characters went still, and into the book, they returned. Alex, wide-eyed with wonder, closed the magical tome.

With a heart full of stories, he felt the warmth of home. 'Thank you,' he whispered, hugging the book tight. Every letter, a friend, every word, pure delight.

Remember, dear reader, just like Alex, you'll see, every story begins with curiosity. So whenever you feel the urge to explore, there's always an adventure, always a door.

A Final Note to Brave Explorer

Dear Adventurer,

You've journeyed through the wilds of the alphabet, met fascinating characters, and discovered the magic in each letter. Remember, every great explorer faces challenges, but it's our courage, curiosity, and determination that help us overcome them.

As you close this book, know that every letter you've met is a friend, cheering you on. You have the power to conquer any word, sentence, or story that comes your way. Keep exploring, keep learning, and remember: the greatest stories are the ones we write ourselves.

Here's to your next adventure in the wonderful world of words!

Warmly,
Zoe Hart

Made in the USA
Las Vegas, NV
30 September 2024

95990115R10021